A MOTHER GOOSE COOKBOOK

PEASE PORRIDGE HOT

written and illustrated by
LORINDA BRYAN CAULEY

G. P. Putnam's Sons New York

For Rob and Lou Bryan—
very special parents

Library of Congress Cataloging in Publication Data
Cauley, Lorinda Bryan. Pease porridge hot.
Summary: A collection of recipes for dishes mentioned
in familiar fairy tales and nursery rhymes.
1. Cookery—Juvenile literature. [1. Cookery] I. Title.
TX652.5.C337   641.5   77-3212
ISBN 0-399-20591-8

INTRODUCTION

Many nursery rhymes and fairy tales passed down through the years mention food or lend themselves to recipe ideas. Here is a collection of storybook recipes and illustrations inspired by some of the best-loved and most well-known tales and rhymes.

This cookbook is for any age child who wants to try out the recipes or simply to look through for the pure enjoyment of the illustrations. The recipes are simple enough for the youngest child to prepare with the guidance of an adult, for his or her friends and family or a special party. The ingredients are for the most part wholesome and nutritious and are presented in a way that can help introduce children to new and healthy foods through a fun idea.

CONTENTS

TIPS TO REMEMBER BEFORE COOKING

1. Ask your mother or father for permission to try a recipe before you begin. Make sure someone will be around while you are cooking in case you have any questions or need any help.

2. Before you start, carefully read over the recipe you plan to use. If you see any unfamiliar words, look them up in the Glossary or ask your mother or father exactly what it means.

3. Gather together all of the ingredients you will need for the recipe you plan to make. Make sure you have all the necessary things before you begin.

4. Wash your hands well with soap and water. Put on an apron if you are wearing something you don't want to get messy.

5. If you will be using the oven, ask someone to preheat it at the correct temperature called for in the recipe. If you need to use the burners, ask someone to show you how to turn them on and how to get different temperatures.

6. Always use a potholder or ovenproof mitt on each hand before removing something hot from the oven or stove.

7. Turn off the burners and oven when you are finished with them.

8. Make sure you clean up your mess when you are done and scrub any pots or pans that you used so that your mother or father will be happy to let you cook again.

HAPPY COOKING!

THE THREE BEARS'
HOT-AND-YUMMY BREAKFAST PORRIDGE

(Enough for Three Hungry Bears)

1¾ cups of water
¼ teaspoon of salt
1 tablespoon of cinnamon
¼ cup of raisins
1⅓ cups of (quick) rolled oats
2 tablespoons of wheat germ
1 cup of milk
honey

1. Pour the water into a saucepan and turn the heat to high. While waiting for it to boil, add the salt, cinnamon, and raisins. When it all starts to bubble hard, add the oats and wheat germ.

2. Turn the heat to low and cook the porridge until all the water is absorbed and the oats are soft (about 3–5 minutes).

3. Pour the porridge into three bowls and cover each with some milk. Dribble some honey over each bowlful, then serve.

4. If the porridge is a little too hot at first, stay close by. You never know when somebody might wander along and eat it all up!

HUMPTY DUMPTY'S
OFF-THE-WALL TOAST

(Enough for Four King's Men)

4 slices of whole wheat (or white) bread
some soft butter
4 eggs
some Parmesan cheese in a shaker
salt and pepper
some parsley flakes

1. Tear out a hole in the center of each piece of bread about the size of a half dollar.

2. Spread each side of the bread with some butter. Turn the heat on under a frying pan and let a small piece of butter melt and sizzle. Spread it around.

3. Place the bread in the pan, and carefully crack an egg over it so that the yolk just lies in the hole. Put as many pieces of bread in at a time as will fit in the pan easily.

4. Allow each piece of bread to brown on one side, then gently flip it over with a turner. When the other side is browned and the egg is fried, remove it from the pan and put it on a plate.

5. Sprinkle it with Parmesan cheese, salt, pepper, and parsley.

THE LITTLE RED HEN'S
QUICK GRAIN OF WHEAT BREAD

(One Delicious Loaf)

2½ cups of whole wheat flour
½ cup of wheat germ
2 teaspoons of baking soda
½ teaspoon of salt
2 cups of buttermilk
2 tablespoons of oil
¼ cup of honey

1. Stir together all of the dry ingredients in a big bowl.

2. Blend the liquid ingredients together, then pour them into the bowl also, and stir well.

3. Grease well a loaf pan. Pour the batter into the pan, scraping the bowl with a spatula. Bake the bread at 325° for 1 hour, or until a toothpick stuck into the middle comes out clean.

4. When it cools down a little, take it out of the pan by turning it upside down into your hand. Put it on a cutting board and see who will help you eat it. It tastes yummy spread with peanut butter and apple butter.

THE BIG BAD WOLF'S
LITTLE PIGS IN A BLANKET

(Enough for Four Famished Wolves)

1 cup of whole wheat flour
(white flour can be used)
2 teaspoons of baking powder
½ teaspoon of salt
2 tablespoons of shortening, such as
butter or margarine
⅓ cup of milk
4 weiners
4 strips of cheddar cheese
4 dill pickle strips
sesame seeds

1. Mix the dry ingredients together in a bowl. Cut in the butter with a fork until it looks like coarse crumbs. Make a well in the middle and pour in the milk. Stir quickly a few times, then form the whole thing into a ball. Now divide this into four small balls.

2. Slice the weiners in half lengthwise. Insert a strip of cheese and a pickle strip in each.

3. Flatten each ball of dough and wrap one around each weiner. Place them on a baking sheet and sprinkle with some sesame seeds. Bake at 400° for 15–20 minutes, or until brown.

4. Fun to make for a lunch, dinner or a party.

THE OWL'S AND THE PUSSYCAT'S
PEA-GREEN SQUASH BOATS

(Four Boats)

2 medium zucchini squash
1 tomato chopped
½ cup of peas
   (fresh, frozen or canned)
1 small onion chopped
½ teaspoon of marjoram
salt and pepper
1 tablespoon of tomato paste
¼ cup of seasoned bread crumbs
¼ cup of Parmesan cheese grated
4 slices of cheese
4 toothpicks

1. Cut the washed zucchini in half lengthwise. With a knife gently cut out the insides leaving at least ¼ inch of the zucchini shell. Carefully scoop it out with a spoon and chop it finely.

2. In a small bowl toss together the chopped squash, the chopped tomato, onion, and peas. Sprinkle in the seasoning, then mix in the tomato paste. Spoon this mixture into the zucchini boats, mounding to fit.

3. Top each boat with the bread crumbs and Parmesan cheese. Place boats in a baking pan side by side. Bake at 350° for 25–30 minutes.

4. Before serving, spear small slices of cheese with a toothpick and stick one in the middle of each boat for a sail.

JACK AND THE BEANSTALK'S
GREEN BEAN CASSEROLE

(Six to Eight Portions)

2 packages of frozen French-style green beans
   (fresh green beans can be used)
1 can of condensed creamed soup
   (chicken, celery, or mushroom)
1 onion chopped
½ cup of slivered almonds
1 can of onion rings

1. Lightly cook the green beans in boiling salted water. Drain, then place in a bowl.

2. Add the can of creamed soup (undiluted), and the chopped onions and almonds to the green beans. Stir it gently together.

3. Pour this mixture into a lightly greased casserole dish. Top it all off with the onion rings, and bake at 350° for 30 minutes.

PETER RABBIT'S
MR. McGREGOR'S GARDEN SALAD

(Enough for Four Hungry Hares)

4 carrots grated
2 stalks of celery chopped
1 large apple sliced in cubes
¼ cup of raisins
¼ cup of chopped walnuts
1 cup of (plain) yogurt mixed with 1 tablespoon of mayonnaise
1 teaspoon of honey
¼ teaspoon of ginger (optional)
lettuce leaves, carrot sticks, extra raisins, nuts, and apple slices
   for decoration

1. Put the grated carrots, chopped celery, sliced apple, raisins, and walnuts in a big bowl. Mix them all together gently. Stir the honey and ginger into the yogurt mixture and pour it over everything. Stir until it is all well coated.

2. Place some lettuce leaves on four dishes. With an ice-cream scoop or large spoon make a mound of the mixture in the middle of each plate.

3. Push two carrot sticks into the top of each mound for rabbit ears. Press raisins in for eyes, a walnut for each nose, and an apple slice for a mouth.

THE COW THAT JUMPED OVER THE MOON'S MOOOOO SHAKE!

(Enough for You and a Friend or Two)

1 cup of buttermilk or plain milk
1 ripe banana
½ cup of apricot nectar or pineapple juice
1 heaping tablespoon of honey
3-4 cubes of ice
a handful of strawberries or blueberries or a ripe peach

1. Put all of the ingredients into the blender at once. Break up the banana and slice the peach if you are using one.

2. Now put the lid on and buzz it all on high until it is smooth and creamy (about 1 minute).

3. Pour the shake into two or three tall glasses and moooooo . . . enjoy!

THE LITTLE OLD WOMAN'S
CATCH-ME-IF-YOU-CAN GINGERBREAD MAN

(One Big One or Two Dozen Small)

½ cup of shortening
½ cup of brown sugar
½ cup of molasses
1 egg
1 tablespoon of vinegar
2½ cups of whole wheat flour
  (white flour can be used)
1 teaspoon of baking soda
¼ teaspoon of salt
1½ teaspoons of ginger
½ teaspoon each of cinnamon
  and cloves

WHITE ICING
2 tablespoons of soft butter
½ cup of confectioner's sugar
¼ teaspoon of vanilla
1 teaspoon of milk
raisins, candies, and nuts for
  decoration

1. Cream together the shortening and sugar, then beat in the molasses, the egg, and the vinegar.

2. Stir the dry ingredients together, then mix them well with the egg-sugar mixture.

3. Form the dough into a big ball, then put it into the refrigerator. Let it chill for 2 or 3 hours.

4. Grease a cookie sheet. Form the gingerbread man by using a small ball for the head and a longer one for the body. Roll some dough into snakes for the arms and legs. Press them into the body and flatten the whole thing down a little with your hand. Bake at 375° for about 20 minutes.

5. When the gingerbread man is done, allow it to cool for 15 minutes. Decorate with icing, raisins for eyes, candies for a mouth, and nuts for buttons. Use the icing for glue to stick them on with. Don't let him get away!

LITTLE RED RIDING HOOD'S
GRANNY'S CUSTARDS
(Makes One Large Custard or Five Small)

**2 cups of milk
3 eggs well-beaten
¼ cup of honey
1 teaspoon of vanilla
a dash of nutmeg**

1. Combine the milk, eggs, honey, and vanilla in a bowl. Pour the mixture into a pitcher with a spout to make it easier to pour into the dishes.

2. Lightly grease five small custard cups or one large baking dish. Pour the egg-milk mixture in evenly. Place them in a pan filled with about one inch of hot water. Sprinkle each with a dash of nutmeg. Put the pan in the oven and bake for 45 minutes at 325° for the small custards, or 1 hour for the large one. You can tell that the custard is set if a knife inserted into the middle comes out clean.

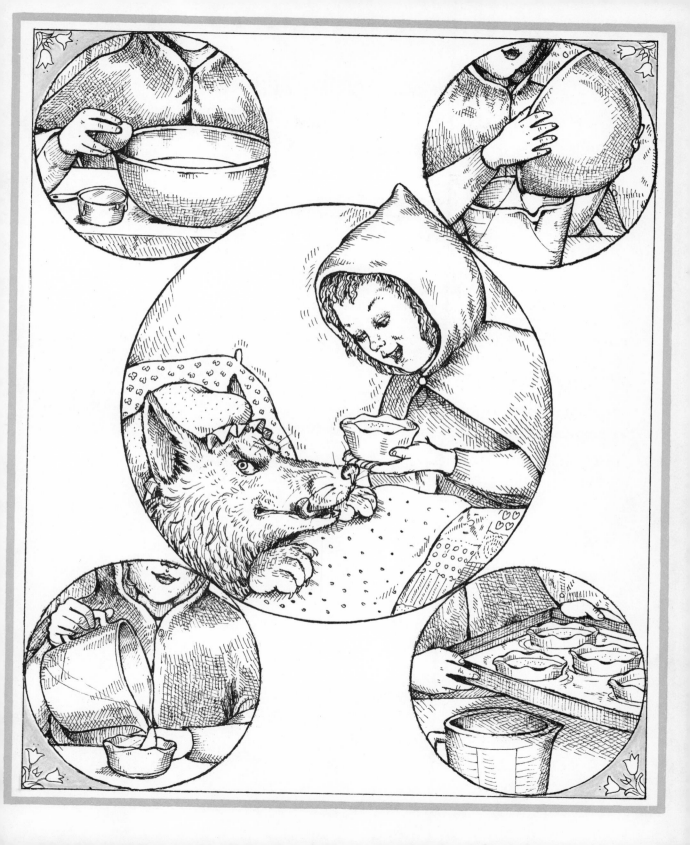

LITTLE MISS MUFFET'S
CURDS AND WHEY WITH FRUIT AND NUTS

(Just Enough for You)

½ cup of cottage cheese
a handful of raisins
5 chopped nuts
1 tablespoon of toasted sunflower seeds
1 sliced peach or orange
1 tablespoon of wheat germ
1 tablespoon of honey

1. Put the cottage cheese into a little bowl. Toss in the raisins, chopped nuts, and sunflower seeds.

2. Slice a peach or orange and arrange it on the cottage cheese. Sprinkle the wheat germ on top and drizzle the honey over it all.

3. Now eat, and don't let any ol' spider frighten you away!

THE QUEEN OF HEARTS'
JAM- AND HONEY-FILLED MERINGUE TARTS

(Makes about Two Dozen)

3 egg whites
1 teaspoon of vanilla
¼ teaspoon of creme of tartar
dash of salt
¾ cup of sugar
strawberry or blackberry jam, or honey and chopped nuts

1. Separate the three eggs. (Store the yolks in a container in the refrigerator for another use.) Let the whites come to room temperature in a bowl (about 10 minutes).

2. Add the vanilla, creme of tartar, and a dash of salt. Beat with a mixer until soft peaks form. Gradually add the sugar and beat until stiff peaks form.

3. Grease a cookie sheet. Drop mixture by tablespoons onto the pan, and using the back of the spoon press a well in the middle of each mound.

4. Bake at 325° for 20 minutes. When cool, remove them from the pan with a metal spatula. Fill each shell with a glob of jam, or a little honey sprinkled with the chopped nuts.

5. Watch out for the Knave of Hearts!

THE THREE LITTLE PIGS'
CINNAMONY, JINNAMONY BAKED APPLES

(Enough for Three Little Pigs and One Wolf)

4 medium-to-large apples
⅓ cup of chopped dates or raisins
¼ cup of brown sugar
4 graham crackers crushed
2 tablespoons of soft butter
1 teaspoon of cinnamon
water (about 1 cup)

1. Wash the apples and remove the seeds and core with a knife or apple corer.

2. Mix the chopped dates or raisins, brown sugar, cracker crumbs, soft butter, and cinnamon together with a fork. Stuff this mixture into each apple center, mounding to fit.

3. Pour the water into a pan and carefully place the apples in next to each other. Shake a little extra cinnamon on each apple. Put the pan in the oven and bake at 350° for about 1 hour.

4. You may want to top the baked apples with a spoonful of vanilla ice cream or yogurt, or pour on some milk before eating.

THE BUN MAN'S
QUICK-AND-EASY HOT CROSS BUNS

(Makes Six Buns)

1 cup of whole wheat flour
(white flour can be used)
2 teaspoons of baking powder
½ teaspoon of salt
2 tablespoons of shortening, such as
butter or margarine
1 tablespoon of honey
½ teaspoon of cinnamon
¼ cup of raisins
⅓ cup of milk

FROSTING
½ cup of confectioner's sugar
2 teaspoons of milk
¼ teaspoon of vanilla

1. Mix the flour, baking powder and salt together in a bowl. Cut in the shortening with a fork until it looks like coarse crumbs. Add the honey, cinnamon and raisins and toss lightly. Make a well in the middle and pour in the milk all at once. Stir it around quickly with a fork and form a ball.

2. Divide the ball into six small ones. Grease a baking sheet and place the six balls on it, about 2 inches apart. With a knife cut a deep cross through the top of each ball. Bake them at 400° for 15–20 minutes.

3. When the rolls are slightly cool, dribble the frosting mixture of confectioner's sugar, milk, and vanilla over each.

THE BILLY-GOATS-GRUFF'S
BANANA PEANUT BUTTER TROLL COOKIES

(Four Dozen Cake-like Cookies)

1 egg beaten
½ cup of honey
¼ cup of brown sugar
1 large (ripe) banana mashed
½ cup of peanut butter
1½ cups of whole wheat flour
   (white flour can be used)
½ teaspoon of baking powder
1 teaspoon of baking soda
½ teaspoon of salt
coconut shreds, nuts, and chocolate chips to decorate

1. Stir together the egg, honey, mashed banana, and peanut butter in a large bowl.

2. Mix the dry ingredients together, then add to the banana mixture. Stir well.

3. Drop by the teaspoonfuls onto a greased cookie sheet about 2 inches apart.

4. Press in two chocolate chips for eyes, a peanut for a nose, and a walnut for a big troll mouth. Arrange chocolate chips around for hair and coconut shreds for a troll beard. Bake at 350° for 10–12 minutes.

HANSEL'S AND GRETEL'S
HEALTHY CHILDREN'S COOKIE HOUSES

(Makes Four Houses)

24 graham cracker squares
a jar of peanut butter
raisins
peanuts
coconut shreds
sunflower seeds
chocolate chips

1. With four graham crackers make a cube, spreading peanut butter on each edge to hold it together. Make four cubes and set them aside.

2. Spread a layer of peanut butter on the tops of the remaining crackers. Decorate these by pressing into them nuts, raisins, sunflower seeds, coconut shreds, and chocolate chips. Two of these crackers will form each roof. Spread one edge of each with peanut butter and make into a tent shape.

3. Spread peanut butter on the top of two opposite crackers of one of the cubes and press the tent-shaped roof on top. Do this with all four cubes.

4. Now you can make windows and doors by decorating the sides with more nuts, raisins, seeds, coconut, and chocolate chips.

THE BAKER'S MAN'S
SUNSHINE ORANGE PAT-A-CAKE

(Serves Nine)

¼ cup of butter, softened
⅔ cup of honey
2 eggs
½ teaspoon of vanilla
2 teaspoons of grated orange peel
2 cups of whole wheat flour
   (white flour can be used)
1 tablespoon of baking powder
½ teaspoon of salt
½ cup of orange juice
confectioner's sugar

SAUCE
½ cup of marmalade
1 tablespoon of butter
2 tablespoons of orange juice
Heat until thick and bubbly.

1. Cream together the butter and honey in a large bowl. Add the eggs and beat until the mixture is slightly fluffy. Add the vanilla and orange peel.

2. In another bowl stir together the flour, baking powder and salt. Add this to the creamed mixture along with the orange juice. Stir until they are mixed, but with as few strokes as you can.

3. Grease a round 8″ cake pan, then dump in a small amount of flour. Shake it around until it coats all of the bottom and sides, then shake out the excess. Pour the cake batter into the pan and bake at 350° for about 30 –40 minutes.

4. Let the cake cool for 10 minutes then remove it from the pan. Put a small handful of confectioner's sugar into a sifter and sift it over the cake, or use the sauce suggested above. If you wish, you can prick your initials on top with a fork.

SIMPLE SIMON'S
FROZEN PIEMAN'S YOGURT PIE

(Serves Six)

1 ¼ cups of graham cracker crumbs
¼ cup of sugar
½ cup of soft butter
1 8-ounce package of cream cheese, softened
1 carton of strawberry or lemon yogurt
1 10-ounce package of sliced strawberries, thawed
fresh strawberries or sliced peaches, if in season

1. Mix the graham cracker crumbs and sugar together in a bowl. Add the softened butter and stir well with a fork until crumbly. Press this mixture into an 8″ or 9″ pie pan. Bake at 400° for 8 minutes.

2. Blend the softened cream cheese with the yogurt in a bowl until it is smooth. Add the strawberries and their syrup to the cheese mixture.

3. When the crust is cool, pour in the filling and carefully put it in the freezer. Before you serve the pie arrange the fresh fruit on top in a pretty design.

LITTLE JACK HORNER'S
PLUM COBBLER PIE

(Six to Eight Servings)

1½ pounds of fresh Italian plums
⅓ cup of water
¾ cup of sugar
2 tablespoons of cornstarch
1 cup of whole wheat flour
   (white flour can be used)
2 tablespoons of sugar
1½ teaspoons of baking powder
¼ teaspoon of salt
¼ cup of butter
¼ cup of milk
1 slightly beaten egg

1. Take the pits out of the plums. Cut them into quarters (about 3 cups) and put them in a saucepan. Add the water and bring to a boil. Let this cook for 3 or 4 minutes.

2. In a small bowl, mix together the sugar and cornstarch. Stir it into the plum mixture. Cook it slowly until it is thick and bubbly, stirring it constantly. Remove it from the heat and pour it into a pie pan.

3. In a bowl, stir together the flour, sugar, baking powder, and salt. Cut in the butter with a fork until it is crumbly.

4. Combine the milk with the slightly beaten egg. Add it all at once to the dry ingredients. Stir it all just enough to moisten everything. Drop this mixture by mounds on top of the plum filling. Bake at 400° for 20–25 minutes.

GLOSSARY

BLEND To thoroughly mix two or more ingredients until they are smooth and not lumpy.

BOIL To cook at boiling temperature (212° at sea level) where bubbles rise to the surface and break.

CHOP To cut into pieces about the size of a pea with a knife or chopper.

CORE To remove the tough middle and seeds by cutting out a circle in the center with a knife or corer, and pulling it out.

CREAM To beat with a spoon or mixer until soft and smooth. With shortening and sugar, they should be beaten until light and fluffy.

CUT IN To mix shortening with dry ingredients using a pastry cutter, knives, or a fork until it looks like coarse crumbs.

GRATE To rub on a grater that separates the food into fine shreds or pieces.

GREASE To rub a pan or dish with shortening until all of the inside edges are coated with a thin layer.

PREHEAT To set the oven at the right temperature before you bake, so that it has time to reach that temperature first.

PRESS A WELL To make a hole in the center of the dough by pressing the middle down with your fingers.

SEPARATE AN EGG To crack an egg by tapping it lightly on the edge of a bowl. Then, holding both ends while pulling them apart, allow the clear whites to drop into the bowl at the same time you catch the yolk in the shell. Carefully pour the whole yolk back and forth between each shell half until all of the white is in the bowl.

SHORTENING   Any fat that can be eaten, such as butter or margarine.

SOFT PEAKS   Egg whites or whipping cream beaten until peaks that curl over form when the beaters are lifted.

STIFF PEAKS   Egg whites beaten until peaks stand up straight when the beaters are lifted, but are still moist and glossy.